Vietnam

Bindu Mathur

First published 1998

Franklin Watts
96 Leonard Street
London EC2A 4RH

0 7496 2941 X

Dewey Decimal Classification Number: 394.2

A CIP catalogue record for this book is available from the British Library

Copyright © 1997 Marshall Cavendish Limited
119 Wardour Street, London W1V 3TD

Marshall Cavendish Limited
Editorial staff
Editorial Director: Ellen Dupont
Art Director: Joyce Mason
Designer: Trevor Vertigan
Sub-Editors: Susan Janes, Judy Fovargue
Production: Craig Chubb
Editorial Assistant: Lorien Kite

Crafts devised and created by Susan Moxley
Music arrangements by Harry Boteler
Photographs by Bruce Mackie
Consultant: Tuyen Nguyen

Printed in Italy

> Adult supervision advised for all crafts and recipes particularly those involving sharp instruments and heat.

CONTENTS

Map of Vietnam 4

Religions and Greetings 6

Ong Tao Festival 8

Tet — New Year's Day 10

Ho Lim Festival 16

Story — Princess My Chau of Co Loa 18

Hung Temple Festival 20

Story — Legend of Lac Long Quan and Lady Au Co 22

Ho Chi Minh's Birthday 24

Vu Lan Day 26

Tet Trung Thu 28

Other Important Festivals 30

Words to Know 31
Index 32

Fiesta! VIETNAM

VIETNAM

Vietnam is a long thin country that stretches along the coast of a peninsula in southeast Asia.

▲ **Ha Long Bay** is in the north of the country. The long coastline of Vietnam has many picturesque island caves and grottoes, as well as beautiful tropical beaches.

◀ **Rice fields** are found all over Vietnam, especially around the River Mekong in the north. Rice is a staple food and is used in many different Vietnamese dishes.

VIETNAM

▲ **Buddha** is worshipped by many Vietnamese people. His image is found in many homes and temples. People also combine Buddhism with the worship of their ancestors.

▶ **City Hall** is one of the most beautiful buildings in the city of Ho Chi Minh in the south of Vietnam. The capital of Vietnam is Hanoi, which is in the north.

RELIGIONS

Vietnam has many religions that have been brought from other countries and cultures. There are also a number of native beliefs that are only found in Vietnam.

BUDDHISM is one of the most popular religions in Vietnam. One in seven Vietnamese is a Buddhist.

Buddhists believe that a young prince named Siddhartha gave up his riches to search for the meaning of life. After years of study the prince became known as Buddha, which means enlightened one.

There are more than 20,000 pagodas dedicated to Buddha in Vietnam. A pagoda is a tower with many levels and is usually found next to a temple. Buddhists go there to worship. They also practise meditation, which is a kind of praying and can be done anywhere.

Buddhist monks, or priests, wear orange or brown-coloured robes and have shaved heads. They usually live in monasteries where they spend their

Village life is important to the Vietnamese people. People of many different religions and ethnic groups come together to the village market with a strong sense of community.

time meditating and studying the Buddhist religion. Their communities are called *sanghas*.

CATHOLICISM is the second biggest religion. There are over six million Catholics in Vietnam. The religion was brought to Vietnam by the French, Spanish and Portuguese.

CAO DAI is the name of a religion found only in Vietnam. It is influenced mainly by Buddhism, Christianity and Confucianism, a Chinese religion. Cao Dai has over two million followers. Another religion native to Vietnam is called Hoa Hao. Both religions come from the southern part of the country.

Vietnamese of all religions usually practise ancestor worship. They pay tribute to family members who have died. Many Vietnamese homes have an altar with pictures of their grandparents and great-grandparents.

GREETINGS FROM VIETNAM!

The population of Vietnam is more than 72 million. There are 54 different ethnic groups, each with a distinct language and culture. The largest group is called the Kinh. They make up almost 80 per cent of the population. Other ethnic groups are the Tay, Thai, Muong, Khmer and Nung.

Vietnamese is the language spoken by most of the population. Many Vietnamese also speak either English, French or Chinese as a second language.

The traditional dress of Vietnam is called the *ao dai*. It is a dress with slits in the sides worn over loose-fitting trousers. Both women and men wear ao dais. For women it is longer, while for men it is shorter and looser. A traditional Vietnamese hat is woven and shaped like a wide cone. It is called a *non la*.

How do you say...

Hello
Chao

Goodbye
Tam Biet

Thank you
Cam On

Peace
Binh An

Fiesta! VIETNAM

Ong Tao Festival

This festival is also known as Le Tao Quan or the Kitchen God Festival. It is celebrated in December before the Vietnamese New Year. It is a time for the family to pay tribute to the Kitchen God.

The Vietnamese think that each family has a spirit that watches over them and their home. This spirit is known as the household or kitchen god.

During Ong Tao each home's kitchen god is replaced by a new one who will look after the family for the coming year. Before he is replaced, the old spirit rides off into the heavens and makes a report to the Jade Emperor. He informs the Jade Emperor about the family's activities for the past year. He also gives details on the state and condition of

This wall decoration can be found hanging in many Vietnamese homes. The long tunic is called an ao dai. *Men wear it with the matching headband especially for the Ong Tao festival.*

Ong Tao Festival

Fresh carp are caught and offered to the household god for Ong Tao. The Vietnamese believe that the god rides the carp to the heavens. If he is happy, he will give a good report to the Jade Emperor.

the home. Families make a special effort to welcome the new god. They want to make sure that he will give a good report to the Jade Emperor at the end of the year.

The house is cleaned from top to bottom. Extra special attention is given to the family altar, with fresh flowers, fruit and incense. People wear paper hats with long flaps on the sides. They also burn gold-coloured paper to honour the household god. Gongs and drums can be heard everywhere in the streets as people play music to welcome the new household god.

Ong Tao is also a time to remember family and friends who have died. The spirits of relatives and loved ones are invited back home to enjoy a meal with the living.

Each family takes extra care to make sure the household god is properly welcomed into the home. Sacrificial gold paper is burned to pay tribute to the household god.

LUNAR CALENDAR

The Ong Tao Festival takes place on the 23rd day of the last lunar month. A lunar month is different from the months used in the West. It is based on the movements of the moon. A lunar month is the time between two new moons which is around 29 days. There are 12 months in a lunar year. Buddhist festivals in Vietnam are based on the lunar calendar.

Fiesta! VIETNAM
TET – NEW YEAR'S DAY

Also known as Tet Nguyen-Dan, this is a New Year celebration marking the first day of the lunar new year. The celebrations last for seven days. It is the largest and most colourful celebration in Vietnam.

Tet is considered to be everybody's birthday. On this day everyone becomes one year older. So if a baby is born one hour before Tet, then only one hour later the child will be two years old!

Tet is traditionally a time for paying visits to family and friends. It is believed that the

GREETING CARDS

All over Vietnam people send greeting cards to friends and family for Tet. It is nice to receive a brightly coloured card that says, "Chuc Mung Nam Moi", or Happy New Year! Here's how you can make your own Tet greeting card. It's so pretty, you might want to send it now!

1 Stretch the cotton fabric over the hoop. Paint the fabric with PVA glue mixed with water and let it dry. Draw your design on white paper in black pen, marking out where the edges are. Trace the design onto the fabric in black ink and colour it in with watercolour paints.

2 Take the thin cardboard and fold into a card. Cut out the rectangular shape in the front where the painted fabric will go. Cut out your design from the fabric and glue it onto the back of the card. Make sure it is seen clearly through the shape in the front.

TET – NEW YEAR'S DAY

first visitor of the New Year to enter the house will bring either good or bad luck for the rest of the year. People often invite a respected person to ensure good fortune for the year.

Celebrations for Tet also take place in public places. All over villages and towns in Vietnam you can see bright lights and paper decorations. Dragon and unicorn dances are also performed in the streets.

YOU WILL NEED
Thin cotton fabric
Thin white cardboard
Watercolour paints
PVA glue
An embroidery hoop

Dragon dances are performed by groups of dancers. If a dragon dances in front of a house, it is good luck. Children and unmarried adults receive gifts of money in red envelopes.

Nem is a pickled pork snack that is considered to be a national delicacy of Vietnam.
Dried fruit and vegetable sweets called mut *are a common sight at Tet. They are very sweet and slightly chewy.*

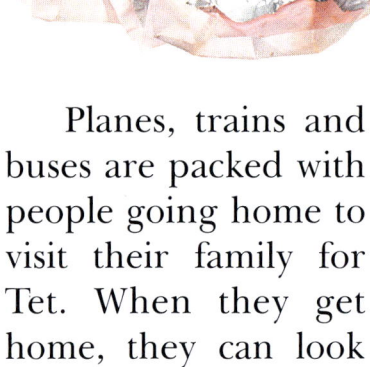

Planes, trains and buses are packed with people going home to visit their family for Tet. When they get home, they can look forward to many festive foods and cakes.

In kitchens all over Vietnam people are busy cooking and preparing delicacies and special dishes for their families.

Children like to eat sweets called *mut* made from dried fruits and vegetables. Another special Tet treat is called *mut hot sen*, or sweetened lotus seeds, which are small and round.

Nem is also popular for the Tet holidays. It is a pickled pork snack with sycamore leaves and it comes wrapped up in green banana leaves. Nem is sold in bunches of five tied on a string and is a common gift for Tet.

The celebration of Tet is not complete without *banh tet* and *banh chung*. They are tasty rice cakes made with meat, beans, and vegetables wrapped and tied in banana leaves. They are then left to cook for up to ten hours.

These rice cakes are a part of many ancient legends. *Banh chung* represents the spirit of Vietnam. They are meant to be eaten in the memory of distant ancestors.

TET – NEW YEAR'S DAY

Spring rolls are also prepared for Tet. They are meat and vegetables wrapped in rice paper. Spring rolls are popular throughout the year all over Vietnam.

Square-shaped rice cake banh chung *is found in the north of Vietnam. The round cake,* banh tet, *is common in the south.*

SPRING ROLLS

MAKES 12

Vegetable oil for stir-frying and deep-frying
225g bean sprouts, rinsed
4 spring onions, very finely chopped
1 leek, finely chopped
1 carrot, grated
100g mushrooms, thinly sliced
2 tbsp soy sauce
½ tsp sugar
½ tsp salt
12 large spring roll wrappers
1 tbsp plain flour mixed to a paste with 1 tbsp water

1 Heat 3–4 tbsp oil in a large frying pan. Add bean sprouts, spring onions, leek, carrot and mushrooms. Stir-fry 1 minute.
2 Stir in soy sauce, sugar and salt. Stir-fry 1 minute longer.
3 Pour vegetables into a sieve in sink. Let drain for 1 hour.
4 Put 2 tbsp vegetable filling on a spring roll wrapper diagonally near a corner. Shape filling into a thin log.
5 Lift the corner flap over the filling and roll once. Fold in both side corners. Roll up. Brush the last flap with the flour paste and press to seal. Make 11 more.
6 Ask an adult to deep-fry the spring rolls in vegetable oil at 180°C. Eat at once, but be careful because the filling is hot.

These are the five fruits of the ngu qua. *They represent the five wishes for the New Year.*

Fresh fruits are also a common sight on any Tet table. It is customary to have the *ngu qua*, or five fruits. These fruits are a banana, a tangerine, an orange, a grapefruit, and a persimmon. They represent five wishes for the New Year. People eat these fruits and hope that their wishes will come true.

People also buy kumquat trees and small orange bushes. They prune them so that they will grow fruit just in time for the Tet festival.

Another common decoration in front of homes is the *Cay Neu* pole. The Cay Neu is a bamboo pole that has been stripped of its leaves. A few leaves are left on top, and the pole is decorated with red paper.

There is an old legend which says that Buddha had made a deal with evil ghosts to stop bothering the people on earth. The ghosts agreed to leave and are only allowed to return to earth for Tet. But Buddha told them they had to stay away from any house with a Cay Neu pole. People put up the Cay Neu to keep their homes safe from evil spirits for Tet.

These are called mai-*apricot blossoms. They are commonly seen in the south of Vietnam. In the north they have* dao-*apricot blossoms, which are pink.*

TET – NEW YEAR'S DAY

PAPER BLOSSOMS

The streets of Vietnam are filled with fragrant and colourful flowers for the Tet festival. People rush to the flower markets to buy spring blossoms to decorate their homes and to give as presents. They believe that flowers make the home more welcoming to good spirits. Other parts of the country have different-coloured blossoms. You can make your own blossoms using a real tree branch and tissue paper to decorate your home or give to someone else.

YOU WILL NEED
Pink or yellow tissue paper
A leafless branch
Green-coloured florist's tape
Scissors

1 Take several sheets of tissue paper and place them on the table stacked together. Cut out the shape seen below through all the thicknesses of the tissue paper. Gather up the bottom flat edge in a bunch and spread the tissue so it looks like a blossom. Tape the bottom in place with the green florist's tape.

2 Find a leafless branch from any tree or bush in your garden. Attach the blossoms onto the branches with the florist's tape.

Fiesta! VIETNAM

HO LIM FESTIVAL

This singing festival takes place two weeks after the Vietnamese New Year. It is held in a village named Lim in the north of Vietnam.

The village of Lim comes alive with music and song during the annual Ho Lim Festival.

People train and practise singing for months in advance. They come from all over Vietnam to take part in the famous singing contest.

The competition takes place between groups of young men and women who are from different villages.

All dressed up in their finest clothes, the singers sit in groups facing each other. Then they begin to sing. The songs are about courtship and love. There are very strict rules about how the songs are sung.

The music never stops during Ho Lim. People keep singing until late in the night. Even when they leave and say goodnight, it is in the form of a song!

There are many other activities that

In the past young men and women went to the Ho Lim Festival to find their future husbands and wives. They sang a type of song called hat doi – a conversation in song.

take place during the festival. People play games like swinging and wrestling. There is a big game of chess with real people acting as the pieces. A tent is also set up for a circus.

Singers practise songs throughout the year while fishing, planting rice or weaving hats and baskets.

NGUOI OI!

Nguoi — oi! Nguoi o — dung ve. — Nguoi — oi! —
— Nguoi o — dung ve. — Nguoi —
ve toi va - ni — co
— may loi nay — nhoi rang — la
doi ben la — ben song — nhu — vat — ao. Ma nay
cung co — a uot dam, — uot dam nhu
mu - a! Nguoi — oi! Nguoi o — dung ve.

Please!
Stay and don't go.
As you leave,
I still have some words
to say.
Leaves change,
one side smooth,
the other rough,
like a dress.
But even they get
soaked with rain.
Please!
Stay and don't go.

PRINCESS MY CHAU OF CO LOA

The Co Loa Festival takes place near Hanoi in January. Local villagers parade in honor of King An Duong Vuong and Princess My Chau. People engage in traditional games and perform folk songs telling the story of their bravery.

THOUSANDS OF YEARS AGO Vietnam was a country called Au Lac, ruled by a great king. The king held court in the capital city of Co Loa. He had only one daughter, a beautiful princess named My Chau. She was famous for wearing a beautiful coat made of thousands of goose feathers.

The king was very popular throughout the land. People respected him for keeping Au Lac safe from all enemies. The king was blessed by the heavens with a magic crossbow. With it he could kill thousands of enemy soldiers with just one single arrow. No other army dared to try to invade the kingdom of Au Lac.

Knowing he could never beat the king, the general of an enemy army decided to make peace. He gave his son, Trong Thuy, to marry the king's daughter. My Chau loved her new husband very much and never wanted to be separated from him. She made a promise to scatter goose feathers from her famous coat so he could find her if they ever lost each other.

But Trong Thuy didn't love the princess. Instead, he stole the magic crossbow to take to his father. Armed with the magic weapon, the general attacked Au Lac. The king tried to fight back, but he was helpless without the magic crossbow. He had to escape with his daughter on horseback. He tried to hide, but the enemy was always right behind them. My Chau had kept her promise to her husband. She had scattered the goose feathers so he could find her. This led the enemy armies right to them.

The king realized this, drew his sword, and killed his daughter. Blood from her slain body poured into the sea. Nourished by the blood of a princess, oysters at the bottom of the sea started producing precious pearls.

Her body finally washed ashore and turned into an enormous stone. Villagers built a temple next to the stone. They still come to the site to pay respects to the princess who was betrayed by her own husband.

Fiesta! VIETNAM

Hung Temple Festival

On this day the Vietnamese celebrate the anniversary of the birth of their ancestors at the Hung Temple in north Vietnam.

The celebrated Hung Temple is located in the north of Vietnam. It was here that the mythical Lady Au Co gave birth to the one hundred eggs that later became the first people of Vietnam.

There are many celebrations that take place at the temple. The festivities begin on the tenth day of the third month of the lunar year, in March.

In ancient times they celebrated the festival with a unicorn dance and many games like tug of war and swinging. People made offerings of rice pies and steamed rice coloured with red and violet dyes.

Today people from all over Vietnam visit the Hung Temple during the festival. They honour the memory of their ancestors and celebrate the origins of their country.

Processions made up of hundreds of people visit the many parts of the Hung

Temple Festivals

There are 20,000 temples in Vietnam. Most of them hold a celebration or festival once a year. In addition to paying tribute to the temple, the festival may honour some historical figure.

People observe these temple festivals by performing special rituals and ceremonies. Outside the temple, people also enjoy themselves by playing games, singing folk songs and watching plays and dance performances. These activities are unique to each temple.

Hung Temple Festival

Temple. They chant, pray and meditate in special ceremonies.

The air is filled with the smell of incense being offered by visitors. Big bronze drums and gongs can be heard everywhere.

Festivities also take place in many nearby villages. There are rowing competitions with dragon boats. People participate in games like swinging and wrestling. Special food stalls sell fresh fruit and local dishes.

The Hung Temple has a Buddhist pagoda called the Thien Quang pagoda. It is famous for its big bell tower. The temple below is called the Ngoc Son Temple. It is found near Hanoi.

LEGEND OF LAC LONG QUAN AND LADY AU CO

At the Hung Temple Festival the Vietnamese pay tribute to Lady Au Co, the Fairy Queen, and Lac Long Quan, the Dragon King. Once upon a time they gave life to a hundred sons at the Hung Temple. The Vietnamese believe these children are their ancestors.

A LONG TIME AGO, before there were any people, there was a strong and fierce dragon who lived beneath the sea. He was called Lac Long Quan and ruled over the oceans. On the land lived the beautiful Lady Au Co. She was so lovely that the wind would sing songs as she walked by. She ruled over the land and was known as the Fairy Queen.

One day the mighty dragon Lac Long Quan emerged from the sea. Huge waves swirled around him as he lifted his mighty body ashore. It was then that he set eyes on the lovely Lady Au Co for the first time.

"I have never before seen such heavenly beauty," he said to the Fairy Queen. Lady Au Co was also overcome with love for the powerful beast. They were married and united their two kingdoms, the sea and the earth, in perfect harmony.

Then Lady Au Co gave birth to a hundred shiny pearl-shelled eggs. These eggs hatched into one hundred strong, healthy sons. The dragon and the Fairy Queen were overjoyed with this rich blessing. They raised their sons with love and care.

After some years Lac Long Quan and Lady Au Co each returned to their kingdoms. Fifty of the sons went with their mother into the mountains of Vietnam. There they became skilled in hunting and in farming the land of the mountains. The other fifty followed their father to the sea. They became skilled fishermen and grew crops in the lowland fields.

So from these pearl eggs of the graceful Lady Au Co and the strong dragon, Lac Long Quan, the very first Vietnamese people were born.

Fiesta! VIETNAM

Ho Chi Minh's Birthday

Ho Chi Minh's birthday is celebrated by the Vietnamese on May 19. They consider him to be the father of their country. All over Vietnam there are events and ceremonies paying tribute to Ho Chi Minh.

Ho Chi Minh became the first president of North Vietnam in 1945. Before that the French ruled Vietnam for many years. Ho Chi Minh led the struggle to make his country independent

HO CHI MINH'S BIRTHDAY

from France. Later on he fought hard to unify Vietnam.

Ho Chi Minh was born in 1890. His real name was Nguyen Tat Thanh. After he became a leader, he changed his name to Ho Chi Minh, which means "he who enlightens".

His birthday is now a national public holiday. Children take part in parades and sports events in honour of the day. Theatres put on plays that tell stories of Ho Chi Minh's life.

At home families place his picture on the wall. They perform a special ceremony to pay respect to Ho Chi Minh. His memory is honoured in other ways throughout the year. Buildings are named after him and one of the largest cities in Vietnam is called Ho Chi Minh City.

Ho Chi Minh was famous for wearing a white helmet like the one shown above. A picture of Ho Chi Minh's house is on page 24. He lived there during World War II.

Fiesta! VIETNAM

VU LAN DAY

Vu Lan takes place in August, in the seventh lunar month. Also known as Wandering Souls Day, it is a time to remember people who have died.

Families spend the day visiting the graves of their loved ones. A special ceremony called *dan chay* is performed at the grave. Incense is burned as an offering to the dead. People believe their souls have left the world and gone to heaven.

Vu Lan is also observed at home. Special offerings are made to the family altar. The altar has two levels. The higher one is devoted to Buddha. The lower level is for deceased relatives.

Offerings of fruit, incense and rice are left on the higher level to please and honour Buddha.

Families remember their loved ones by placing rice soup and fruit on the second level of the altar. Another offering is called the *tan sinh*, which is fish, meat and

Chanting beads, Chinese incense sticks and this small wooden drum are all used for Vu Lan.

VU LAN DAY

shrimp, representing three living creatures. The *ngu qua*, or five fruits, should also be placed on the family altar. Dishes of puffed rice and boiled sweet potatoes are placed in every room for the souls of deceased family members.

Special paper is burned for Vu Lan. People believe it helps to subdue any lost or wandering souls.

But Vu Lan is not a sad time. There are many celebrations in Buddhist temples and homes. It is a time to cherish and honour the memory of those who have died.

This wooden banana tree is a decoration adorning many Vietnamese homes. It is sometimes placed on the family altar.

BAKED BANANAS

1 Preheat the oven to 190°C/375°F/Gas 5. Lightly grease a large ovenproof dish with a little of the butter.
2 Put the butter and sugar in a mixing bowl. Using a wooden spoon, beat until creamy.
3 Beat in the cloves, orange juice, lemon juice and ground ginger.
4 Arrange the bananas in a single layer in the prepared dish. Spread the butter mixture over the bananas. Put dish in oven. Bake for 10–15 minutes until topping is bubbling.
5 To serve, spoon the bananas and juices on to plates.

MAKES 6
50g butter, at room temperature
200g soft brown sugar
¼ tsp ground cloves
2 tbsp orange juice
1 tsp lemon juice
¼ tsp ground ginger
6 bananas, sliced lengthways

Fiesta! VIETNAM

TET TRUNG THU

This festival is also known as the Children's or Harvest Festival. It takes place during the eighth lunar month, in late September, when the full moon is at its brightest.

Tet Trung Thu used to celebrate the beginning of the harvest. Now it is a festival for children to gather in the streets and celebrate under the full moon.

On this day you'll find the streets filled with processions of children singing to the beat of loud drums and gongs.

They also carry candles and lanterns. The lanterns come in many different shapes and sizes. There are tigers, dragons, lions and unicorns. Today the lanterns are also made with modern designs, such as boats, aeroplanes and cars. All over Vietnam, children

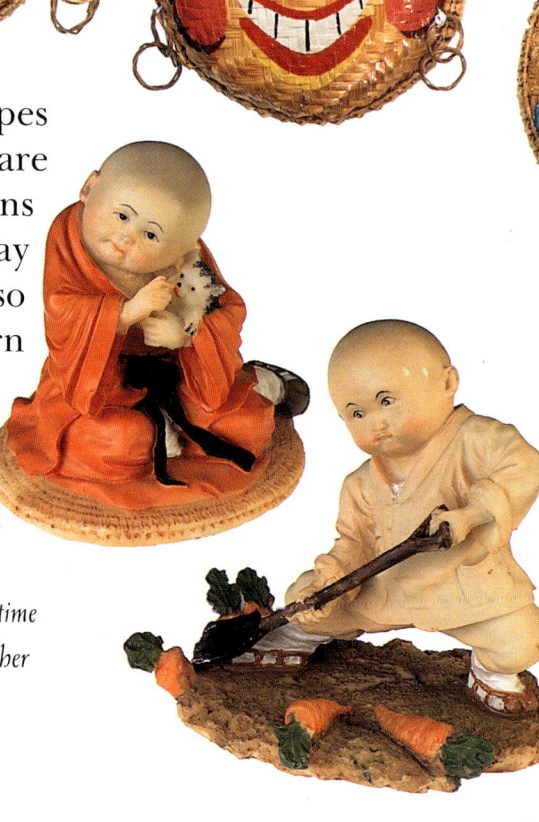

This child is harvesting rice in time for the Harvest Festival. The other is a follower of Buddha.